The Usborne Book of
Poems
for
Young Children

The Usborne Book of

Poems
for
Young Children

Chosen by Philip Hawthorn

Illustrated by Cathy Shimmen

Edited by Sam Taplin

Contents

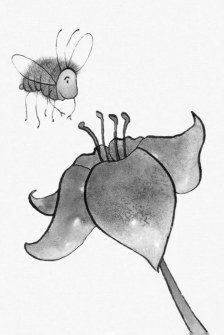

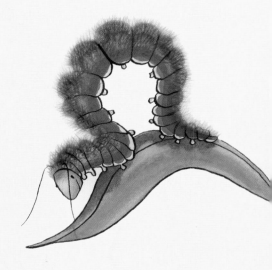

Introduction

Choosing a collection of poems like this is
a tricky job. Imagine throwing a party to
which you can invite anyone at all, but only
having room for a hundred guests. Like all the
best parties, I wanted this book to be fun and
surprising, so there's a good mix of old poems
and new ones, long poems and short ones,
and a whole variety of styles. There's also a
huge range of subjects, from ketchup to kiwis.

I hope you enjoy reading the poems as
much as I enjoyed choosing them.

Philip Hawthorn

Magic Cat

My mum whilst walking through the door
Spilt some magic on the floor.
Blobs of this
and splots of that
but most of it upon the cat.

Our cat turned magic, straight away
and in the garden went to play
where it grew two massive wings
and flew around in fancy rings.
"Oh look!" cried Mother, pointing high,
"I didn't know our cat could fly."
Then with a dash of Tibby's tail
she turned my mum into a snail!

So now she lives beneath a stone
and dusts around a different home.
And I'm an ant
and Dad's a mouse
And Tibby's living in our house.

Peter Dixon

Spring

Sound the Flute!
Now it's mute.
Birds delight
Day and Night;
Nightingale
In the dale,
Lake in Sky,
Merrily,
Merrily, Merrily to welcome in the Year.

Little Boy
Full of joy;
Little Girl,
Sweet and small;
Cock does crow,
So do you;
Merry voice,
Infant noise,
Merrily, Merrily to welcome in the Year.

Little Lamb,
Here I am;
Come and lick
My white neck;
Let me pull
Your soft Wool;
Let me kiss
Your soft face:
Merrily, merrily, we welcome in the year.

William Blake

The Caterpillar

Brown and furry
Caterpillar in a hurry;
Take your walk
To the shady leaf or stalk.

May no toad spy you,
May the little birds pass by you;
Spin and die,
To live again a butterfly.

Christina Rossetti

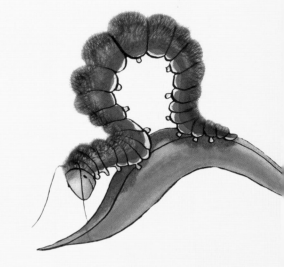

What Do You Suppose?

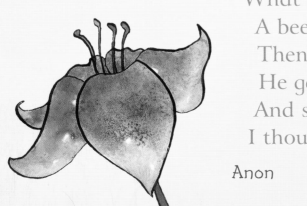

What do you suppose?
A bee sat on my nose.
Then what do you think?
He gave me a wink
And said, "I beg your pardon,
I thought you were the garden."

Anon

The Animals Went in Two by Two

The animals went in two by two,
Hurrah! Hurrah!
The animals went in two by two,
The elephant and the kangaroo,
And they all went into the ark
For to get out of the rain.

The animals went in three by three,
Hurrah! Hurrah!
The animals went in three by three,
The wasp, the ant and the bumble bee,
And they all went into the ark
For to get out of the rain.

The animals went in four by four,
Hurrah! Hurrah!
The animals went in four by four,
The great hippopotamus stuck in the door,
And they all went into the ark
For to get out of the rain...

Anon

Rain

There are holes in the sky
Where the rain gets in,
But they're ever so small,
That's why rain is thin.

Spike Milligan

Weather

Whether the weather be fine
Or whether the weather be not,
Whether the weather be cold
Or whether the weather be hot,
We'll weather the weather
Whatever the weather,
Whether we like it or not.

Anon

Pennies from Heaven

I put 10p in my Piggy Bank
To save for a rainy day.
It rained the *very next morning!*
Three Cheers, Hip Hip Hooray!

Spike Milligan

The Snowman

Once there was a snowman
Stood outside the door,
Thought he'd like to come inside
And run around the floor;
Thought he'd like to warm himself
By the firelight red;
Thought he'd like to clamber up
On that big white bed.
So he called the North Wind, "Help me now I pray.
I'm completely frozen, standing here all day."
So the North Wind came along and blew him in the door –
And now there's nothing left of him
But a puddle on the floor.

Anon

Haiku

Snowman in a field
listening to the raindrops
wishing him farewell

Roger McGough

from The Pied Piper of Hamelin

Into the street the Piper stept,
Smiling first a little smile,
As if he knew what magic slept
In his quiet pipe the while;
Then, like a musical adept,
To blow the pipe his lips he wrinkled,
And green and blue his sharp eyes twinkled,
Like a candle-flame where salt is sprinkled;
And ere three shrill notes the pipe uttered
You heard as if an army muttered;
And the muttering grew to a grumbling;
And the grumbling grew to a mighty rumbling;
And out of the houses the rats came tumbling,

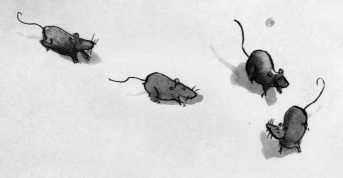

Great rats, small rats, lean rats, brawny rats,
Brown rats, black rats, grey rats, tawny rats,
Grave old plodders, gay young friskers,
Fathers, mothers, uncles, cousins,
Cocking tails and pricking whiskers,
Families by tens and dozens,
Brothers, sisters, husbands, wives –
Followed the Piper for their lives.
From street to street he piped advancing,
And step for step they followed dancing...

Robert Browning

17

Choosing their Names

Our old cat has kittens three –
What do you think their names should be?

One is a tabby with emerald eyes,
And a tail that's long and slender,
And into a temper she quickly flies
If you ever by chance offend her.
I think we shall call her this –
I think we shall call her that –
Now, don't you think that **Pepperpot**
Is a nice name for a cat?

One is black with a frill of white,
And her feet are all white fur,
If you stroke her she carries her tail upright
And quickly begins to purr.
I think we shall call her this –
I think we shall call her that –
Now, don't you think that Sootikin
Is a nice name for a cat?

One is a tortoiseshell yellow and black,
With plenty of white about him;
If you tease him, at once he sets up his back,
He's a quarrelsome one, ne'er doubt him.
I think we shall call him this —
I think we shall call him that —
Now don't you think that Scratchaway
Is a nice name for a cat?

Our old cat has kittens three
And I fancy these their names will be:
Pepperpot, Sootikin, Scratchaway — there!
Were ever kittens with these to compare?
And we call the old mother —
Now, what do you think? —
Tabitha Longclaws Tiddley Wink.

Thomas Hood

19

The Sound of the Wind

The wind has such a rainy sound
Moaning through the town,
The sea has such a windy sound, –
Will the ships go down?

The apples in the orchard
Tumble from their tree. –
Oh will the ships go down, go down,
In the windy sea?

Christina Rossetti

When Lamps are Lighted
in the Town

When lamps are lighted in the town
The boats sail out to sea.
The fishers watch when night comes down,
They watch for you and me.

You little children go to bed,
Before you sleep I pray
That God will watch the fishermen
And bring them home at day.

Anon

On the Ning Nang Nong

On the Ning Nang Nong
Where the Cows go Bong!
And the Monkeys all say Boo!
There's a Nong Nang Ning
Where the trees go Ping!
And the tea pots Jibber Jabber Joo.
On the Nong Ning Nang
All the mice go Clang!
And you just can't catch 'em when they do!
So it's Ning Nang Nong!
Cows go Bong!
Nong Nang Ning!
Trees go Ping!
Nong Ning Nang!
The mice go Clang!
What a noisy place to belong,
Is the Ning Nang Ning Nang Nong!!

Spike Milligan

22

A Good Play

We built a ship upon the stairs
All made of the back-bedroom chairs,
And filled it full of sofa pillows
To go a-sailing on the billows.

We took a saw and several nails,
And water in the nursery pails;
And Tom said, "Let us also take
An apple and a slice of cake;"
Which was enough for Tom and me
To go a-sailing on, till tea.

We sailed along for days and days,
And had the very best of plays;
But Tom fell out and hurt his knee,
So there was no one left but me.

Robert Louis Stevenson

The Sound Collector

A stranger called this morning
Dressed all in black and grey
Put every sound into a bag
And carried them away

The whistling of the kettle
The turning of the lock
The purring of the kitten
The ticking of the clock

The popping of the toaster
The crunching of the flakes
When you spread the marmalade
The scraping sound it makes

The hissing of the frying-pan
The ticking of the grill
The bubbling of the bathtub
As it starts to fill

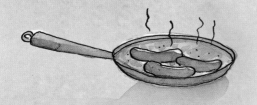

24

The drumming of the raindrops
On the window-pane
When you do the washing-up
The gurgle of the drain

The crying of the baby
The squeaking of the chair
The swishing of the curtain
The creaking of the stair

A stranger called this morning
He didn't leave his name
Left us only silence
Life will never be the same.

Roger McGough

The Eagle

He clasps the crag with crooked hands;
Close to the sun in lonely lands,
Ring'd with the azure world, he stands.

The wrinkled sea beneath him crawls;
He watches from his mountain walls,
And like a thunderbolt he falls.

Alfred Tennyson

A Man on a Length of Elastic

A man on a length of elastic
Decided to do something drastic.
When he jumped off the cliff he
Came back in a jiffy
And screamed to his friends, "It's fantastic!"

Michael Palin

Kite

A kite on the ground
Is just paper and string
but up in the air
it will dance and sing.
A kite in the air
will dance and caper
but back on the ground
is just string and paper.

Anon

Until I Saw the Sea

Until I saw the sea
I did not know
that wind
could wrinkle water so.

I never knew
that sun
could splinter a whole sea of blue.

Nor
did I know before,
a sea breathes in and out
upon a shore.

Lilian Moore

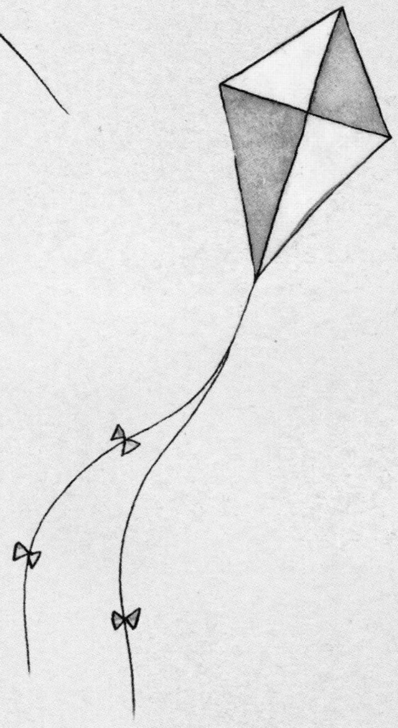

Grim and Gloomy

Oh, grim and gloomy,
So grim and gloomy
Are the caves beneath the sea.
Oh, rare but roomy
And bare and boomy,
Those salt sea caverns be.

Oh, slim and slimy
Or grey and grimy
Are the animals of the sea.
Salt and oozy
And safe and snoozy
The caves where these animals be.

Hark to the shuffling,
Huge and snuffling,
Ravenous, cavernous, great sea-beasts!
But fair and fabulous,
Tintinnabulous,
Gay and fabulous are their feasts.

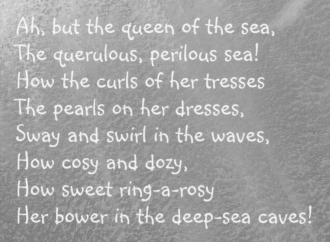

Ah, but the queen of the sea,
The querulous, perilous sea!
How the curls of her tresses
The pearls on her dresses,
Sway and swirl in the waves,
How cosy and dozy,
How sweet ring-a-rosy
Her bower in the deep-sea caves!

Oh, rare but roomy
And bare and boomy
Those caverns under the sea,
And grave and grandiose,
Safe and sandiose
The dens of her denizens be.

James Reeves

A Baby Sardine

A baby sardine
Saw her first submarine:
She was scared and watched through a peephole.

"Oh come, come, come,"
Said the sardine's mum,
"It's only a tin full of people."

Spike Milligan

The Quangle Wangle's Hat

On top of the Crumpetty Tree
The Quangle Wangle sat,
But his face you could not see,
On account of his Beaver Hat.
For his Hat was a hundred and two feet wide,
With ribbons and bibbons on every side,
And bells, and buttons, and loops, and lace,
So that nobody ever could see the face
Of the Quangle Wangle Quee.

The Quangle Wangle said
To himself on the Crumpetty Tree,
"Jam; and jelly; and bread;
Are the best of food for me!
But the longer I live on this Crumpetty Tree,
The plainer than ever it seems to me
That very few people come this way,
And that life on the whole is far from gay!"
Said the Quangle Wangle Quee.

But there came to the Crumpetty Tree
Mr and Mrs Canary;
And they said, "Did you ever see
Any spot so charmingly airy?
May we build a nest on your lovely Hat?
Mr Quangle Wangle, grant us that!
O please let us come and build a nest
Of whatever material suits you best,
Mr Quangle Wangle Quee!"

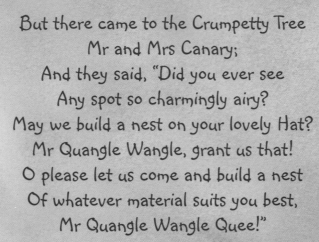

And besides, to the Crumpetty Tree
Came the Stork, the Duck and the Owl;
The Snail and the Bumble-Bee,
The Frog, and the Fimble Fowl
(The Fimble Fowl with a corkscrew leg);
And all of them said, "We humbly beg,
We may build our homes on your lovely Hat,
Mr Quangle Wangle, grant us that!
Mr Quangle Wangle Quee!"

And the Golden Grouse came there,
And the Pobble who has no toes,
And the small Olympian Bear
And the Dong with a luminous nose.
And the Blue Baboon, who played the flute,
And the Orient Calf from the land of Tute,
And the Attery Squash and the Bisky Bat,
All came and built on the lovely Hat
Of the Quangle Wangle Quee.

And the Quangle Wangle said
To himself on the Crumpetty Tree,
"When all these creatures move
What a wonderful noise there'll be!"
And at night by the light of the Mulberry Moon
They danced to the Flute of the Blue Baboon
On the broad green leaves of the Crumpetty Tree,
And all were as happy as happy could be,
With the Quangle Wangle Quee.

Edward Lear

Montague Michael

Montague Michael
You're much too fat,
You wicked old, wily old,
Well-fed cat.

All night you sleep
On a cushion of silk,
And twice a day
I bring you milk.

And once in a while,
When you catch a mouse,
You're the proudest person
In all the house.

But spoilt as you are,
I tell you sir,
This dolly is mine
And you can't have her!

Anon

As
I Was
Going
up the Stair

As I was going up the stair
I met a man who wasn't there.
He wasn't there again today –
Oh, how I wish he'd go away.

Anon

The Elephant

Elephants are useful friends,
Equipped with handles at both ends,
They have a wrinkled moth-proof hide,
Their teeth are upside-down, outside,
If you think the elephant preposterous,
You've probably never seen a rhinosterous.

Ogden Nash

The Tortoise

Come crown my brow with leaves of myrtle,
I know the tortoise is a turtle,
Come carve my name in stone immortal,
I know the turtoise is a tortle.
I know to my profound despair,
I bet on one to beat a hare,
I also know I'm now a pauper,
Because of its tortley, turtley, torpor.

Ogden Nash

The Lion

The lion is the king of beasts,
And husband of the lioness.
Gazelles and things on which he feasts
Address him as your highoness.
There are those that admire that roar of his,
In the African jungles and velds,
But, I think that wherever the lion is,
I'd rather be somewhere else.

Ogden Nash

An Imaginary Menagerie

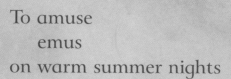

To amuse
       emus
on warm summer nights

       Kiwis
do wiwis
from spectacular heights.

Roger McGough

Windy Nights

Whenever the moon and stars are set,
Whenever the wind is high,
All night long in the dark and wet,
A man goes riding by.
Late in the night when the fires are out,
Why does he gallop and gallop about?

Whenever the trees are crying aloud,
And ships are tossed at sea,
By, on the highway, low and loud,
By at the gallop goes he.
By at the gallop he goes, and then
By he comes back at the gallop again.

Robert Louis Stevenson

Mrs Moon

Mrs Moon
sitting up in the sky
Little Old Lady
rock-a-bye
with a ball of fading light
and silvery needles
knitting the night.

Roger McGough

maggie and milly and molly and may

maggie and milly and molly and may
went down to the beach (to play one day)

and maggie discovered a shell that sang
so sweetly she couldn't remember her troubles, and

milly befriended a stranded star
whose rays five languid fingers were;

and molly was chased by a horrible thing
which raced sideways while blowing bubbles: and

may came home with a smooth round stone
as small as a world and as large as alone.

For whatever we lose (like a you or a me)
it's always ourselves that we find in the sea

E.E.Cummings

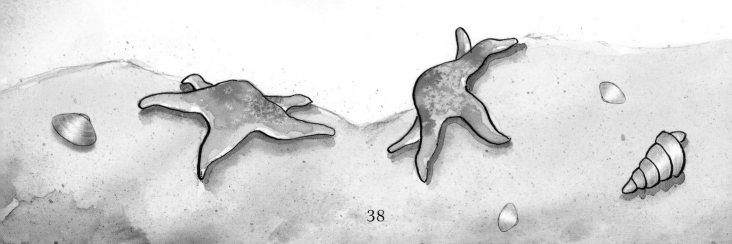

Seaing the Sea

knee deep in the ocean
something in the ever-steady knee-cap lapping
motion
of the ocean
moves me to emotion
something infinitely playful
something totally and finally benign
in the briny
makes these four eyes of mine wet with weep
(as if there wasn't enough salt water already
in the deep blue)

John Hegley

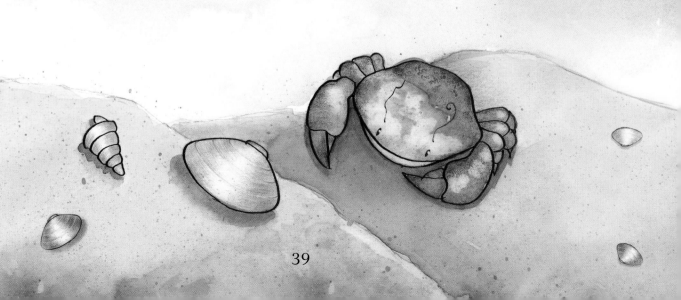

The Owl and the Pussy-cat

The Owl and the Pussy-cat went to sea
In a beautiful pea-green boat,
They took some honey, and plenty of money,
Wrapped up in a five-pound note.
The Owl looked up to the stars above,
And sang to a small guitar,
"O lovely Pussy! O Pussy, my love
What a beautiful Pussy you are,
You are,
You are!
What a beautiful Pussy you are!"

Pussy said to the Owl, "You elegant fowl!
How charmingly sweet you sing!
O let us be married! Too long we have tarried:
But what shall we do for a ring?"
They sailed away, for a year and a day,
To the land where the Bong-tree grows,
And there in a wood a Piggy-wig stood
With a ring at the end of his nose,
His nose,
His nose,
With a ring at the end of his nose.

"Dear Pig, are you willing to sell for one shilling
Your ring?" Said the Piggy, "I will."
So they took it away, and were married next day
By the Turkey who lives on the hill.
They dined on mince, and slices of quince,
Which they ate with a runcible spoon;
And hand in hand, on the edge of the sand,
They danced by the light of the moon,
The moon,
The moon,
They danced by the light of the moon.

Edward Lear

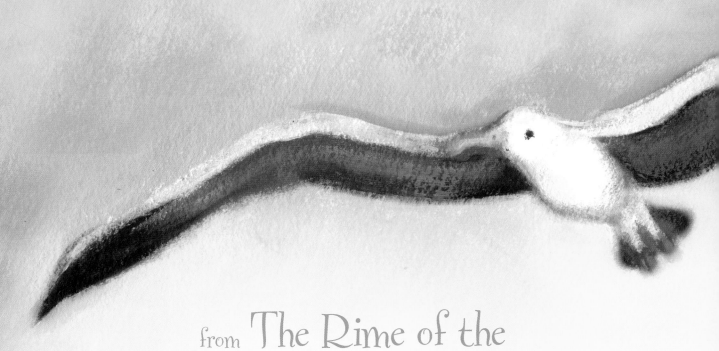

from The Rime of the Ancient Mariner

And now there came both mist and snow,
And it grew wondrous cold:
And ice, mast-high, came floating by,
As green as emerald.

And through the drifts the snowy clifts
Did send a dismal sheen:
Nor shapes of men nor beasts we ken –
The ice was all between.

The ice was here, the ice was there,
The ice was all around:
It cracked and growled, and roared and howled,
Like noises in a swound!

At length did cross an Albatross,
Thorough the fog it came;
As if it had been a Christian soul,
We hailed it in God's name.

It ate the food it ne'er had eat,
And round and round it flew.
The ice did split with a thunder-fit;
The helmsman steered us through!

And a good south wind sprung up behind;
The Albatross did follow,
And every day, for food or play,
Came to the mariner's hollo!

In mist or cloud, on mast or shroud,
It perched for vespers nine;
Whiles all the night, through fog-smoke white,
Glimmered the white Moon-shine.

"God save thee, ancient Mariner!
From the fiends, that plague thee thus! –
Why look'st thou so?" – "With my cross-bow
I shot the ALBATROSS."

Samuel Taylor Coleridge

The Swing

How do you like to go up in a swing,
Up in the air so blue?
Oh, I do think it the pleasantest thing
Ever a child can do!

Up in the air and over the wall,
Till I can see so wide,
Rivers and trees and cattle and all
Over the countryside -

Till I look down on the garden green,
Down on the roof so brown —
Up in the air I go flying again,
Up in the air and down!

Robert Louis Stevenson

Rain in Summer

How beautiful is the rain!
After the dust and the heat,
In the broad and fiery street,
In the narrow lane,
How beautiful is the rain!

How it clatters along the roofs
Like the tramp of hoofs,
How it gushes and struggles out
From the throat of the overflowing spout!

Across the window-pane
It pours and pours;
And swift and wide,
With a muddy tide,
Like a river down the gutter roars
The rain, the welcome rain!

Henry Wadsworth Longfellow

I'm Glad the Sky is Painted Blue

I'm glad the sky is painted blue,
And the earth is painted green,
With such a lot of nice fresh air
All sandwiched in between.

Anon

Be Like the Bird

Be like the bird who,
Resting in his flight
On a twig too slight,
Feels it bend beneath him
Yet sings,
Knowing he has wings.

Victor Hugo

Bed in Summer

In winter I get up at night
And dress by yellow candle-light.
In summer, quite the other way,
I have to go to bed by day.

I have to go to bed and see
The birds still hopping on the tree,
Or hear the grown-up people's feet
Still going past me in the street.

And does it not seem hard to you,
When all the sky is clear and blue,
And I should like so much to play,
To have to go to bed by day?

Robert Louis Stevenson

A Man Said to Me

A man said to me,
"Can you sing?"
I said, "Sing?"
He said, "Yes."
I said, "Who?"
He said, "You."
I said, "Me?"
He said, "Yes."
I said, "When?"
He said, "Now."
I said, "Now?"
He said, "Yes."
I said, "No."
He said, "Oh."

Anon

My Shadow

I have a little shadow that goes in and out with me,
And what can be the use of him is more than I can see.
He is very, very like me from the heels up to the head;
And I see him jump before me, when I jump into my bed.

The funniest thing about him is the way he likes to grow –
Not at all like proper children, which is always very slow;
For he sometimes shoots up taller like an india-rubber ball,
And he sometimes gets so little that there's none of him at all.

He hasn't got a notion of how children ought to play,
And can only make a fool of me in every sort of way,
He stays so close beside me, he's a coward you can see;
I'd think shame to stick to nursie as that shadow sticks to me!

One morning, very early, before the sun was up,
I rose and found the shining dew on every buttercup;
But my lazy little shadow, like an arrant sleepy-head,
Had stayed at home behind me and was fast asleep in bed.

Robert Louis Stevenson

The Brook

I come from haunts of coot and hern,
I make a sudden sally,
And sparkle out among the fern,
To bicker down a valley.

By thirty hills I hurry down,
Or slip between the ridges,
By twenty thorps, a little town,
And half a hundred bridges.

Till last by Philip's farm I flow
To join the brimming river,
For men may come and men may go,
But I go on for ever.

I chatter over stony ways,
In little sharps and trebles,
I bubble into eddying bays,
I babble on the pebbles.

With many a curve my banks I fret
By many a field and fallow,
And many a fairy foreland set
With willow-weed and mallow.

I chatter, chatter, as I flow
To join the brimming river,
For men may come and men may go,
But I go on for ever.

I wind about, and in and out,
With here a blossom sailing,
And here and there a lusty trout,
And here and there a grayling.

And here and there a foamy flake
Upon me, as I travel
With many a silvery waterbreak
Above the golden gravel,

And draw them all along, and flow
To join the brimming river,
For men may come and men may go,
But I go on for ever.

I steal by lawns and grassy plots,
I slide by hazel covers;
I move the sweet forget-me-nots
That grow for happy lovers.

I slip, I slide, I gloom, I glance,
Among my skimming swallows;
I make the netted sunbeam dance
Against my sandy shallows.

I murmur under moon and stars
In brambly wildernesses;
I linger by my shingly bars;
I loiter round my cresses;

And out again I curve and flow
To join the brimming river,
For men may come and men may go,
But I go on for ever.

Alfred Tennyson

Betty Botter

Betty Botter bought some butter,
But, she said, this butter's bitter;
If I put it in my batter,
It will make my batter bitter,
But a bit of better butter
Will make my batter better.
So she bought a bit of butter
Better than her bitter butter,
And she put it in her batter,
And the batter wasn't bitter.
So, 'twas better Betty Botter
Bought a bit of better butter.

Anon

Peter Piper

Peter Piper picked a peck of pickled pepper;
Did Peter Piper pick a peck of pickled pepper?
If Peter Piper picked a peck of pickled pepper,
Where's the peck of pickled pepper Peter Piper picked?

Anon

She Sells Sea-shells

She sells sea-shells on the sea shore;
The shells that she sells are sea-shells I'm sure.
So if she sells sea-shells on the sea shore,
I'm sure that the shells are sea-shore shells.

Anon

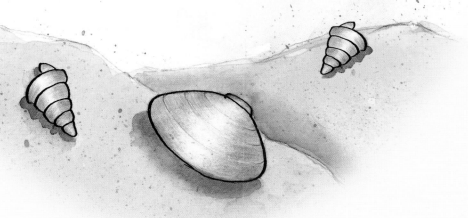

The Train from Loch Brane

There once was a driver
Called Hamish McIver,
Who drove the fast train
From Perth to Loch Brane.
For years he had driven
The route he'd been given,
But one day he thought he'd
Be ever so naughty.

So next Monday morning,
Without any warning,
He went off the rails
And headed for Wales.
It gave all his passengers
Quite a big challenge, as
Where they were going,
They'd no way of knowing.

But round about three
They arrived at the sea,
And Hamish bought everyone
Welsh cakes and tea.
And when they had snacked,
He trundled them back,
Through fields and forest
And railway track.

And after all shouting,
"Hooray for the outing!"
The people all said,
As they climbed into bed,
That Hamish McIver's
The very best driver
Who ever drove trains
From Perth to Loch Brane…
From Perth to Loch Brane…
From Perth to Loch Brane…
From Perth to Loch Brane…

Philip Hawthorn

Five Little Owls

Five little owls in an old elm tree,
Fluffy and puffy as owls could be,
Blinking and winking with big round eyes
At the big round moon that hung in the skies:
As I passed beneath I could hear one say,
"There'll be mouse for supper, there will, today!"
Then all of them hooted, "Tu-whit, tu-whoo
Yes, mouse for supper, hoo-hoo, hoo-hoo!"

Anon

Algy

Algy met a bear,
A bear met Algy.
The bear was bulgy,
The bulge was Algy.

Anon

The Old Man of St. Bees

There was an old man of St. Bees,
Who was stung on the arm by a wasp,
When asked, "Does it hurt?"
He replied, "No, it doesn't,
I'm so glad it wasn't a hornet."

W. S. Gilbert

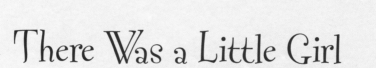

There Was a Little Girl

There was a little girl, who had a little curl
Right in the middle of her forehead,
And when she was good, she was very, very good,
But when she was bad she was horrid.

Henry Wadsworth Longfellow

No Harm Done

As I was going out one day
My head fell off and rolled away.
But when I saw that it had gone,
I picked it up and put it on.

And when I got into the street
A fellow cried, "Look at your feet!"
I looked at them and sadly said,
"I've left them both asleep in bed!"

Anon

The Old Man of Peru

There was an old man of Peru,
Who dreamt he was eating his shoe;
He awoke in the night
With a terrible fright,
And found it was perfectly true.

Anon

The Dentist and the Crocodile

The crocodile, with cunning smile, sat in the dentist's chair.
He said, "Right here and everywhere my teeth require repair."
The dentist's face was turning white. He quivered, quaked and shook.
He muttered, "I suppose I'm going to have to take a look."
"I want you," Crocodile declared, "to do the back ones first.
The molars at the very back are easily the worst."
He opened wide his massive jaws. It was a fearsome sight –
At least three hundred pointed teeth, all sharp and shining white.
The dentist kept himself well clear. He stood two yards away.
He chose the longest probe he had to search out the decay.
"I said to do the back ones first!" the Crocodile called out.
"You're much too far away, dear sir, to see what you're about.
To do the back ones properly, you've got to put your head
Deep down inside my great big mouth," the grinning Crocky said.
The poor old dentist wrung his hands and, weeping from despair,
He cried, "No no! I see them all extremely well from here!"
Just then, in burst a lady, in her hands a golden chain.
She cried, "Oh Croc, you naughty boy, you're playing tricks again!"
"Watch out!" the dentist shrieked and started climbing up the wall.
"He's after me! He's after you! He's going to eat us all!"
"Don't be a twit," the lady said, and flashed a gorgeous smile.
"He's harmless. He's my little pet, my lovely crocodile."

Roald Dahl

Have You Ever Seen?

Have you ever seen a duvet on a flower bed?
Or a single hair from a hammer's head?
Has the foot of a mountain got any toes?
And can you cross over the bridge of a nose?

Why don't the hands on a clock ever clap?
Or the wings of a building flutter or flap?
Can the bottoms of oceans sit down for their tea?
And can you unlock the trunk of a tree?

Are the teeth of a comb ever going to bite?
Can the eye of a needle look left – and then right?
Has the bank of a river ever got any cash?
And how loud is the sound of a computer's crash?

Anon, adapted by Philip Hawthorn

Strange Story

I saw a pigeon making bread
I saw a girl composed of thread
I saw a towel one mile square
I saw a meadow in the air
I saw a rocket walk a mile
I saw a pony make a file
I saw a blacksmith in a box
I saw an orange kill an ox
I saw a butcher made of steel
I saw a penknife dance a reel
I saw a sailor twelve feet high
I saw a ladder in a pie
I saw an apple fly away
I saw a sparrow making hay
I saw a farmer like a dog
I saw a puppy mixing grog
I saw three men who saw these too
And will confirm what I tell you.

Anon

(Hint: Try reading the first half
of a line and then the second
half of the line above it.)

Children with Adults

My auntie gives me a colouring book and crayons.
I begin to colour.
After a while she looks over to see what I have done and says
you've gone over the lines
that's what you've done.
What do you think they're there for, ay?
Some kind of statement is it?
Going to be a rebel are we?
I begin to cry.
My uncle gives me a hanky and some blank paper
do your own designs he says
I begin to colour.
When I have done he looks over and tells me they are all very good.
He is lying,
only some of them are.

John Hegley

An Owner's Complaint

I've got a dog that's more
like a carrot than a dog.
It's hairy,
but only very slightly,
it's got no personality
to speak of,
no bark to bark of,
no head,
no legs,
no tail,
and it's all
orange
and
crunchy

John Hegley

Witches' Chant
from Macbeth

Round about the cauldron go:
In the poisoned entrails throw.
Toad, that under cold stone
Days and nights has thirty-one
Sweated venom sleeping got,
Boil thou first in the charmèd pot.
Double, double toil and trouble;
Fire burn and cauldron bubble.

Fillet of a fenny snake,
In the cauldron boil and bake;
Eye of newt and toe of frog,
Wool of bat and tongue of dog,
Adder's fork and blindworm's sting,
Lizard's leg and owlet's wing.
For a charm of powerful trouble,
Like a hell-broth boil and bubble.
Double, double toil and trouble;
Fire burn and cauldron bubble.

Scale of dragon, tooth of wolf,
Witch's mummy, maw and gulf
Of the ravenous salt-sea shark,
Root of hemlock digged in the dark.
Add thereto a tiger's chaudron,
For the ingredients of our cauldron.
Double, double toil and trouble;
Fire burn and cauldron bubble.

William Shakespeare

There Was an Old Woman

There was an old woman who swallowed a fly,
I don't know why she swallowed a fly –
Perhaps she'll die...

There was an old woman who swallowed a spider,
It wriggled and jiggled and wiggled inside her.
She swallowed the spider to catch the fly,
I don't know why she swallowed the fly –
Perhaps she'll die...

There was an old woman who swallowed a bird,
How absurd, to swallow a bird!
She swallowed the bird to catch the spider
That wriggled and jiggled and wiggled inside her,
She swallowed the spider to catch the fly,
I don't know why she swallowed the fly –
Perhaps she'll die...

There was an old woman who swallowed a cat,
Fancy that – she swallowed a cat!
She swallowed the cat to catch the bird,
She swallowed the bird to catch the spider
That wriggled and jiggled and wiggled inside her,
She swallowed the spider to catch the fly,
I don't know why she swallowed the fly –
Perhaps she'll die...

There was an old woman who swallowed a dog,
What a hog, to swallow a dog!
She swallowed the dog to catch the cat,
She swallowed the cat to catch the bird,
She swallowed the bird to catch the spider
That wriggled and jiggled and wiggled inside her,
She swallowed the spider to catch the fly,
I don't know why she swallowed the fly –
Perhaps she'll die...

There was an old woman who swallowed a cow,
I don't know how she swallowed a cow.
She swallowed the cow to catch the dog,
She swallowed the dog to catch the cat,
She swallowed the cat to catch the bird,
She swallowed the bird to catch the spider
That wriggled and jiggled and wiggled inside her,
She swallowed the spider to catch the fly,
I don't know why she swallowed the fly –
Perhaps she'll die...

There was an old woman who swallowed a horse.
(She's dead, of course.)

Anon

From a Railway Carriage

Faster than fairies, faster than witches,
Bridges and houses, hedges and ditches,
And charging along like troops in a battle,
All through the meadows, the horses and cattle:
All of the sights of the hill and the plain
Fly as thick as driving rain;
And ever again, in the wink of an eye,
Painted stations whistle by.

Here is a child who clambers and scrambles,
All by himself and gathering brambles;
Here is a tramp who stands and gazes;
And there is the green for stringing the daisies!
Here is a cart run away in the road,
Lumping along with man and load;
And here is a mill, and there is a river;
Each a glimpse and gone for ever!

Robert Louis Stevenson

Little Trotty Wagtail

Little trotty wagtail he went in the rain
And tittering tottering sideways he ne'er got straight again,
He stooped to get a worm and look'd up to catch a fly,
And then he flew away ere his feathers they were dry.

Little trotty wagtail he waddled in the mud,
And left his little foot marks, trample where he would.
He waddled in the water pudge and waggle went his tail,
And chirrupt up his wings to dry upon the garden rail.

Little trotty wagtail you nimble all about,
And in the dimpling water pudge you waddle in and out;
Your home is nigh at hand and in the warm pigsty,
So, little Master Wagtail, I'll bid you a goodbye.

John Clare

The Jumblies

They went to sea in a Sieve, they did,
In a Sieve they went to sea:
In spite of all their friends could say,
On a winter's morn, on a stormy day,
In a Sieve they went to sea!
And when the Sieve turned round and round,
And everyone cried, "You'll all be drowned!"
They called aloud, "Our Sieve ain't big,
But we don't care a button! We don't care a fig!
In a Sieve we'll go to sea!"
Far and few, far and few,
Are the lands where the Jumblies live;
Their heads are green, and their hands are blue,
And they went to sea in a Sieve.

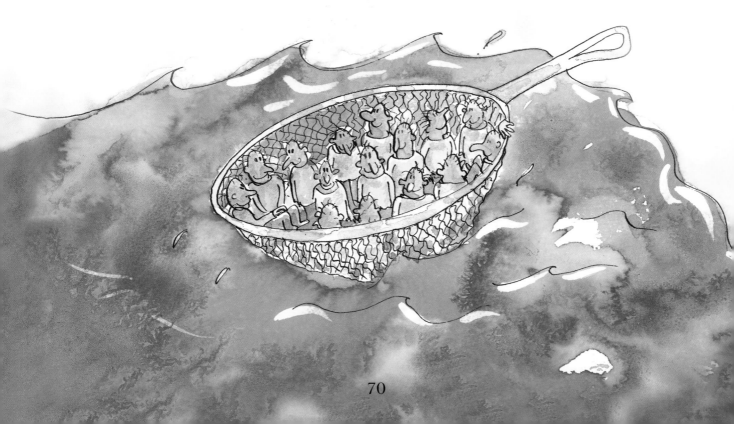

They sailed away in a Sieve, they did,
In a Sieve they sailed so fast,
With only a beautiful pea-green veil
Tied with a riband by way of a sail,
To a small tobacco-pipe mast;
And everyone said, who saw them go,
"Oh won't they be soon upset, you know!
For the sky is dark, and the voyage is long,
And happen what may, it's extremely wrong
In a Sieve to sail so fast!"
Far and few, far and few,
Are the lands where the Jumblies live;
Their heads are green, and their hands are blue,
And they went to sea in a Sieve.

The water it soon came in, it did,
The water it soon came in;
So to keep them dry, they wrapped up their feet
In a pinky paper all folded neat,
And they fastened it down with a pin.
And they passed the night in a crockery-jar,
And each of them said, "How wise we are!
Though the sky be dark, and the voyage be long,
Yet we never can think we were rash or wrong,
While round in our Sieve we spin!"
Far and few, far and few,
Are the lands where the Jumblies live;
Their heads are green, and their hands are blue,
And they went to sea in a Sieve.

And all night long they sailed away;
And when the sun went down,
They whistled and warbled a moony song
To the echoing sound of a coppery gong,
In the shade of the mountains brown.
"O Timballoo! How happy we are,
When we live in a Sieve and a crockery-jar,
And all night long in the moonlight pale,
We sail away with a pea-green sail,
In the shade of the mountains brown!"
Far and few, far and few,
Are the lands where the Jumblies live;
Their heads are green, and their hands are blue,
And they went to sea in a Sieve.

They sailed to the Western Sea, they did,
To a land all covered with trees,
And they bought an Owl, and a useful Cart,
And a pound of Rice, and a Cranberry Tart,
And a hive of silvery Bees.
And they bought a Pig, and some green Jackdaws,
And a lovely Monkey with lollipop paws,
And forty bottles of Ring-Bo-Ree,
And no end of Stilton Cheese.
Far and few, far and few,
Are the lands where the Jumblies live;
Their heads are green, and their hands are blue,
And they went to sea in a Sieve.

And in twenty years they all came back,
In twenty years or more,
And everyone said, "How tall they've grown!
For they've been to the Lakes, and the Torrible Zone,
And the hills of the Chankly Bore";
And they drank their health, and gave them a feast
Of dumplings made of beautiful yeast;
And everyone said, "If we only live,
We too will go to sea in a Sieve,
To the hills of the Chankly Bore!"
Far and few, far and few,
Are the lands where the Jumblies live;
Their heads are green, and their hands are blue,
And they went to sea in a Sieve.

Edward Lear

An Accident

An accident happened to my brother Jim
When somebody threw a tomato at him —
Tomatoes are juicy and don't hurt the skin,
But this one was specially packed in a tin.

Anon

Peas

I eat my peas with honey,
I've done it all my life;
It makes the peas taste funny,
But it keeps them on the knife.

Spike Milligan

On Tomato Ketchup

If you do not shake the bottle,
None'll come, and then a lot'll.

Anon

Ask Mummy Ask Daddy

When I ask Daddy
Daddy says ask Mummy

When I ask Mummy
Mummy says ask Daddy.
I don't know where to go.

Better ask my teddy
he never says no.

John Agard

Don't Call Alligator Long-mouth Till You Cross River

Call alligator long-mouth
call alligator saw-mouth
call alligator pushy-mouth
call alligator scissors-mouth
call alligator raggedy-mouth
call alligator bumpy-bum
call alligator all dem rude word
but better wait
                till you cross river.

John Agard

Queen Nefertiti

Spin a coin, spin a coin,
All fall down;
Queen Nefertiti
Stalks through the town.

Over the pavements
Her feet go clack,
Her legs are as tall
As a chimney stack;

Her fingers flicker
Like snakes in the air,
The walls split open
At her green-eyed stare;

Her voice is thin
As the ghosts of bees;
She will crumble your bones,
She will make your blood freeze.

Spin a coin, spin a coin,
All fall down;
Queen Nefertiti
Stalks through the town.

Anon

The Cats of Kilkenny

There once were two cats of Kilkenny.
Each thought there was one cat too many;
So they fought and they fit,
And they scratched and they bit;
Till, except for their nails
And the tips of their tails,
Instead of two cats, there weren't any.

Anon

The Wizard of Oz

The fabulous Wizard of Oz
Retired from business because
What with up-to-date science,
To most of his clients,
He wasn't the Wizard he woz.

Anon

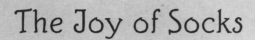

The Joy of Socks

Nice warm socks,
Nice warm socks –
We should celebrate them.
Ask a toe!
Toes all know
It's hard to overrate them.

Toes say, "Please
Don't let us freeze
Till we're numb and white.
Summer's gone
Put them on!
Wear them day and night!"

Nice warm socks,
Nice warm socks –
Who would dare to mock them?
Take good care
Of every pair
And never, ever knock them.

Wendy Cope

The Sorrow of Socks

Some socks are loners –
They can't live in pairs.
On washdays they've shown us
They want to be loners.
They puzzle their owners,
They hide in dark lairs.
Some socks are loners
They won't live in pairs.

Wendy Cope

Friends

Funky monkey in the tree
I like it when you talk to me
What I really like the best
Is when you bang upon my chest.

Slippery snake I am your mate
When all others hesitate
I'll be there right by your side
I am known to slip and slide.

Hop along, croak croak, how ya doing frog?
No one understands our deep dialogue
People may laugh when they see us on the road
We must stick together
Monkey, snake, me, you and toad.

Benjamin Zephaniah

Classrhymes

Tony's bony,
Paul is tall,
Billy's silly,
Deborah's...er...

Pete's been to Crete,
Hugh to Peru,
Erica to America,
Deborah to...er...

Claire has fair hair,
Mark is dark,
Wanda's blonde,
Dave is shaved —

Ned is red,
Jack is black,
Clyde is dyed,
Deborah is...er...

Jane likes Wayne,
Wally likes Polly,
Stew likes Sue,
Deborah likes...er...

Mike has a bike,
Doug has a bug,
Pat has a cat,
Deborah has...a zebra!

Philip Hawthorn

80

The Girl in the Choir

There was a young girl in the choir,
Whose voice rose higher and higher;
Till one Sunday night,
It rose quite out of sight,
And they found it next day on the spire.

Anon

A Fellow Called Green

There was a young fellow called Green,
Whose musical sense wasn't keen;
He said, "It is odd,
But I cannot tell *God
Save the Weasel* from *Pop Goes the Queen*."

Anon

W

The King sent for his wise men all
To find a rhyme for W;
When they had thought a good long time
But could not think of a single rhyme,
"I'm sorry," said he, "to trouble you."

James Reeves

Tarantella

Do you remember an Inn, Miranda?
Do you remember an Inn?
And the tedding and the shredding
Of the straw for a bedding,
And the fleas that tease in the High Pyrenees,
And the wine that tasted of tar?
And the cheers and the jeers of the young muleteers
(Under the vine of the dark veranda)?
Do you remember an Inn, Miranda,
Do you remember an Inn?
And the cheers and the jeers of the young muleteers
Who hadn't got a penny,
And who weren't paying any,
And the hammer at the doors and the din?
And the hip! hop! hap!
Of the clap
Of the hands to the swirl and the twirl
Of the girl gone chancing,
Glancing,
Dancing,
Backing and advancing,
Snapping of the clapper to the spin
Out and in —
And the ting, tong, tang of the guitar!
Do you remember an Inn, Miranda?
Do you remember an Inn?

Never more;
Miranda,
Never more.
Only the high peaks' hoar;
And Aragon a torrent at the door.
No sound
In the walls of the halls where falls
The tread
Of the feet of the dead to the ground,
No sound:
But the boom
Of the far waterfall like doom.

Hilaire Belloc

The Hairy Toe

Once there was a woman went out to pick beans,
and she found a Hairy Toe.
She took the Hairy Toe home with her,
and that night, when she went to bed,
the wind began to moan and groan.
Away off in the distance
she seemed to hear a voice crying,
"Where's my Hair-r-ry To-o-oe?
Who's got my Hair-r-ry To-o-oe?"

The woman scrooched down,
'way under the covers,
and about that time
the wind appeared to hit the house,
smoosh
and the old house creaked and cracked
like something was trying to get in.
The voice had come nearer,
almost at the door now,
and it said,
"Where's my Hair-r-ry To-o-oe?
Who's got my Hair-r-ry To-o-oe?"

The woman scrooched further down
under the covers
and pulled them tight around her head.
The wind growled around the house
like some big animal
and r-r-um-mbled
over the chimbley.
All at once she heard the door cr-r-a-ck
and Something slipped in
and began to creep over the floor.

The floor went
cre-e-eak, cre-e-eak
at every step that thing took towards her bed.
The woman could almost feel
it bending over her bed.
Then in an awful voice it said:
"Where's my Hair-r-ry To-o-oe?
Who's got my Hair-r-ry To-o-oe?
You've got it!"

Anon

85

Is the Moon Tired?

Is the moon tired? She looks so pale
Within her misty veil;
She scales the sky from east to west,
And takes no rest.

Before the coming of the night
The moon shows papery white;
Before the dawning of the day
She fades away.

Christina Rossetti

The Star

Twinkle, twinkle, little star,
How I wonder what you are!
Up above the world so high,
Like a diamond in the sky.

When the blazing sun is gone,
When he nothing shines upon,
Then you show your little light,
Twinkle, twinkle, all the night.

Then the traveller in the dark,
Thanks you for your tiny spark,
He could not see which way to go,
If you did not twinkle so.

In the dark blue sky you keep,
And often through my curtains peep,
For you never shut your eye,
Till the sun is in the sky.

As your bright and tiny spark,
Lights the traveller in the dark –
Though I know not what you are,
Twinkle, twinkle, little star.

Jane Taylor

A Fellow Named Paul

There was a young fellow named Paul,
Who went to a fancy dress ball.
He thought he would risk it
And go as a biscuit,
But a dog ate him up in the hall.

Anon

The Cheerful Old Bear

A cheerful old bear at the zoo
Could always find something to do;
When it bored him to go
On a walk to and fro,
He reversed it, and went fro and to.

Anon

The Lady of Venice

There was a young lady of Venice
Who used hard-boiled eggs to play tennis.
When they said, "It is wrong,"
She replied, "Go along!
You don't know how prolific my hen is!"

Anon

The Woman in High Heels

A woman in high heels from Twickenham
Was late, so she had to walk quick in 'em.
But it made her feel funny
All over her tummy,
So she took 'em right off and was sick in 'em.

Anon

See You Later!

See you later, alligator.
In a while, crocodile.
See you later, hot potato.
If you wish, jelly-fish.
Not too soon, you big baboon.
Toodle-oo, kangaroo.
Bye-bye, butterfly.
See you tomorrow, horror.
In a week, freak.

Anon

Wynken, Blynken and Nod

Wynken, Blynken and Nod one night
Sailed off in a wooden shoe –
Sailed on a river of crystal light,
Into a sea of dew.
"Where are you going, and what do you wish?"
The old moon asked the three.
"We have come to fish for the herring fish
That live in this beautiful sea;
Nets of silver and gold have we!"
Said Wynken,
Blynken,
And Nod.

The old moon laughed and sang a song,
As they rocked in the wooden shoe,
And the wind that sped them all night long
Ruffled the waves of dew.
The little stars were the herring fish
That lived in that beautiful sea –
"Now cast your nets wherever you wish –
Never afeard are we";
So cried the stars to the fishermen three:
Wynken,
Blynken,
And Nod.

All night long their nets they threw
To the stars in the twinkling foam –
Then down from the skies came the wooden shoe,
Bringing the fishermen home;
'Twas all so pretty a sail it seemed
As if it could not be,
And some folks thought 'twas a dream they'd dreamed
Of sailing that beautiful sea –
But I shall name you the fishermen three:
Wynken,
Blynken,
And Nod.

Wynken and Blynken are two little eyes,
And Nod is a little head,
And the wooden shoe that sailed the skies
Is the wee one's trundle-bed.
So shut your eyes while mother sings
Of wonderful sights that be,
And you shall see the beautiful things
As you rock in the misty sea,
Where the old shoe rocked the fishermen three:
Wynken,
Blynken,
And Nod.

Eugene Field

Young Night Thought

All night long, and every night,
When my mamma puts out the light,
I see the people marching by,
As plain as day, before my eye.

Armies and emperors and kings,
All carrying different kinds of things,
And marching in so grand a way,
You never saw the like by day.

So fine a show was never seen
At the great circus on the green;
For every kind of beast and man
Is marching in that caravan.

At first they move a little slow,
But still the faster on they go,
And still beside them close I keep
Until we reach the town of Sleep.

Robert Louis Stevenson

Sweet and Low

Sweet and low, sweet and low,
Wind of the western sea,
Low, low, breathe and blow,
Wind of the western sea!
Over the rolling waters go,
Come from the dying moon, and blow,
Blow him again to me;
While my pretty one, while my pretty one, sleeps.

Sleep and rest, sleep and rest,
Father will come to thee soon;
Rest, rest, on mother's breast,
Father will come to thee soon;
Father will come to his babe in the nest,
Silver sails all out of the west
Under the silver moon:
Sleep, my little one, sleep, my pretty one, sleep.

Alfred Tennyson

Index of First Lines

Acknowledgements

Every effort has been made to trace the copyright holders of the material in this book. If any rights have been omitted, the publishers offer to rectify this in any subsequent editions following notification. The publishers are grateful to the following organizations and individuals for their permission to reproduce copyright material.

8 "Magic Cat" by Peter Dixon, taken from Macmillan's *The Works*, 2000. Reprinted by permission of Pan Macmillan.

14 "Rain" and "Pennies from Heaven" by Spike Milligan. Reprinted by permission of Spike Milligan Productions Ltd.

15 "Haiku" by Roger McGough. Reprinted by permission of PFD on behalf of: Roger McGough. ©1983 by Roger McGough: as printed in the original volume.

22 "On the Ning Nang Nong" by Spike Milligan. Reprinted by permission of Spike Milligan Productions Ltd.

24 "The Sound Collector" by Roger McGough. Reprinted by permission of PFD on behalf of: Roger McGough. ©1992 by Roger McGough.

26 "A Man on a Length of Elastic" from *Limericks* by Michael Palin, published by Hutchinson. Reprinted by permission of the Random House Group Limited.

27 "Until I Saw the Sea" by Lilian Moore. Reprinted by permission of Marian Reiner Literary Agency on behalf of Lilian Moore. ©1967 Lilian Moore.

28 "Grim and Gloomy" by James Reeves. ©James Reeves, from *Complete Poems for Children* (Classic Mammoth). Reprinted by permission of the James Reeves estate.

29 "A Baby Sardine" by Spike Milligan. Reprinted by permission of Spike Milligan Productions Ltd.

34 "The Elephant" and "The Tortoise" by Ogden Nash. ©1950 by Ogden Nash. Reprinted by permission of Curtis Brown, Ltd.

35 "The Lion" by Ogden Nash. ©1950 by Ogden Nash. Reprinted by permission of Curtis Brown, Ltd.

35 "An Imaginary Menagerie" by Roger McGough. Reprinted by permission of PFD on behalf of: Roger McGough. ©Roger McGough.

37 "Mrs Moon" by Roger McGough. Reprinted by permission of PFD on behalf of: Roger McGough. ©1983 Roger McGough.

38 "maggie and milly and molly and may" is reprinted from *Complete Poems 1904-1962*, by E.E.Cummings, edited by George J. Firmage, by permission of WWNorton and company, Copyright ©1991 by the Trustees for the E.E.Cummings Trust and George James Firmage.

39 "Seaing the Sea" by John Hegley. Reprinted by permission of PFD on behalf of: John Hegley. ©John Hegley.

54 "The Train from Loch Brane" by Philip Hawthorn. Reprinted by permission of the author. ©Philip Hawthorn.

57 "The Old Man of St. Bees" by W.S.Gilbert. Reprinted by permission of the Royal Theatrical Fund.

59 "The Dentist and the Crocodile" from *Rhyme Stew* by Roald Dahl. Copyright ©1989 by Roald Dahl. Reprinted by permission of Viking Kestrel, a division of Penguin Young Readers Group, a member of Penguin Group (USA) Inc., 345 Hudson Street, New York, NY 10014, and of Jonathan Cape Ltd. All rights reserved.

60 "Have You Ever Seen?", adapted by Philip Hawthorn. This version ©2004 Philip Hawthorn. Reprinted by permission of Philip Hawthorn.

62 "Children with Adults" by John Hegley. Reprinted by permission of PFD on behalf of: John Hegley. ©John Hegley.

63 "An Owner's Complaint" by John Hegley. Reprinted by permission of PFD on behalf of: John Hegley. ©John Hegley.

74 "Peas" by Spike Milligan. Reprinted by permission of Spike Milligan Productions Ltd.

75 "Ask Mummy Ask Daddy" by John Agard. Reprinted by kind permission of John Agard c/o Caroline Sheldon Literary Agency. From *Say it again Granny*, published by Bodley Head (1989).

75 "Don't Call Alligator Long-mouth Till You Cross River" by John Agard. Reprinted by kind permission of John Agard c/o Caroline Sheldon Literary Agency. From *I din do Nuttin*, published by Bodley Head (1991).

78 "The Joy of Socks" and "The Sorrow of Socks" by Wendy Cope. Reprinted by permission of PFD on behalf of: Wendy Cope. ©Wendy Cope.

79 "Friends" by Benjamin Zephaniah. Reprinted by permission of PFD on behalf of: Benjamin Zephaniah. ©Benjamin Zephaniah.

80 "Classrhymes" by Philip Hawthorn. Reprinted by permission of the author. ©Philip Hawthorn.

81 "W" by James Reeves. ©James Reeves, from *Complete Poems for Children* (Classic Mammoth). Reprinted by permission of the James Reeves estate.

82 "Tarantella" by Hilaire Belloc. Reprinted by permission of PFD on behalf of The Estate of Hilaire Belloc. ©1970 by The Estate of Hilaire Belloc.

Additional illustrations by Katie Lovell
Designed by Melissa Orrom Swan and Francesca Allen